FRANKLIN PARK PUBLIC LIBRARY
FRANKLIN PARK, IL.

Who Was Louis Braille?

Who Was
Louis Braille?

by Margaret Frith
illustrated by Robert Squier

Grosset & Dunlap
An Imprint of Penguin Random House

For Luther—MF

For my grandfather, painter Donald G. Squier, whose passion
to create never faltered—even when his eyesight failed—RS

GROSSET & DUNLAP
Penguin Young Readers Group
An Imprint of Penguin Random House LLC

ISBN 978-0-448-47903-3

10 9 8 7 6

Contents

Who Was
Louis Braille?

When Louis Braille was three years old, he had a terrible accident that left him blind. But being blind did not stop Louis from having a happy childhood. Living in the dark made him even more curious about the world around him. He was a bright, good-natured boy. He also had a remarkable memory. He couldn't read or write. But at the school in the small French village where he lived, he could listen and remember. He was one of the best students.

At the age of ten, Louis went off to Paris to study at the only school for blind children in France. The library had fourteen books for the blind that were printed with embossed, or raised, letters. The blind read them with their fingers.

Louis couldn't wait to have books he could read by himself. But reading the library books wasn't easy. Each letter was so large that the reader had to trace it with many fingers. The reader also had to remember all the letters that had gone before to figure out a single word. Large letters meant large pages. The books were very long and weighed as much as nine pounds! Only a few of the boys could get through them. Louis was one of them.

Then he found out about something called "night writing." Louis was excited. It used a code of raised dots instead of embossed letters. But he found that night writing had problems, too.

The answer was to invent his own system.

Louis worked for three years on his reading and writing code. By the time he was fifteen, he had figured it out.

Today, almost two hundred years later, the whole world still uses this same system called *braille.* The blind have been forever grateful to Louis Braille, an unselfish, determined young man.

There is a marble plaque in honor of Louis Braille at the family home in Coupvray, France. It says

IN THIS HOUSE

ON JANUARY 4 1809 WAS BORN

LOUIS BRAILLE

INVENTOR OF THE SYSTEM OF

WRITING IN RAISED DOTS FOR USE

BY THE BLIND.

HE OPENED THE DOORS OF

KNOWLEDGE TO ALL THOSE

WHO CANNOT SEE.

Chapter 1
The Accident

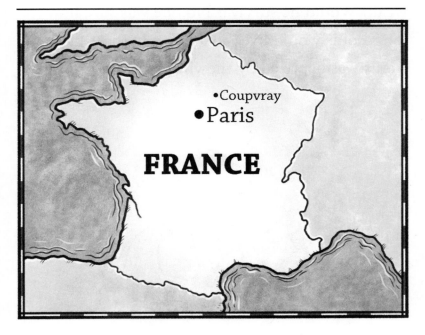

Coupvray
Paris

FRANCE

In 1809, on January 4, Louis Braille was born in Coupvray, France. Coupvray is a small farming village twenty-five miles from the bustling city of Paris.

Louis's mother showed the new baby to his sisters and brother. Louis looked so tiny in his mother's arms. Monique and Simon-René worried about their new son. He was so small, and he was weak. Would he survive? No one was sure how long Louis would live. So after only three days, Louis was baptized by the village priest.

His mother and father needn't have worried.
With all their care, Louis grew into a happy,
healthy boy with blue eyes and curly blond hair.
As soon as he could walk, he was running out into
the fields, his mother chasing after him. His sisters
and brother, who were much older, loved playing
with little Louis.

The family lived in a simple house on ten acres of land. They kept a cow for fresh milk and chickens for eggs. They had a vegetable garden and fruit trees, and a small vineyard.

The Brailles were not rich, but they worked hard and made a good living.

Louis's mother looked after the family and the garden.

Louis's father spent his days in a workshop
across from the house. He was a harness and
saddle maker, as his father had been. He worked
in leather, making reins, bridles, and saddles.

Louis helped his mother in the garden and
gathered eggs from the nesting boxes. But what
he loved most was going to the workshop with
his father.

Simon-René spent most of the time at his workbench. While his father cut and stitched

pieces of leather, Louis sat nearby and played with
the leftover scraps.

Sometimes his father plunked Louis down on a fancy saddle and Louis pretended to ride.

Louis was fascinated with all the tools on the bench. One day while his father stepped away for a moment, Louis picked up one of the sharp tools. He tried to punch a hole in a piece of leather. But the tool slid on the slippery surface and pierced Louis's eye.

Louis cried out in terrible pain! His parents came running. What were they to do? The closest doctor was many miles away in another town. However, in Coupvray there was a woman who cared for the sick. The woman came and bathed Louis's eye with lily water. But the damage was done. Louis would never see out of that eye. To make matters worse, the infection spread to Louis's other eye. As the days passed, his world grew darker. By the time he was four, Louis was completely blind.

Chapter 2
The Village School

In France in the early nineteenth century, blind children from poor families often ended up on the streets, begging. Louis was lucky to have a father and mother who could take good care of him.

His father carved him a wooden cane. Louis began tapping his way everywhere—indoors and out.

Simon-René also looked for things Louis could do with his hands. He taught him how to make fringes for harnesses.

His parents were determined that Louis learn to read and write. His father made an alphabet with nails arranged in the shape of letters pounded into a board. Louis traced the letters with his fingers. It wasn't long before he knew them all. No one was surprised. Louis was a fast learner.

Father Jacques Palluy, the village priest, was friends with the Braille family. He saw that Louis was a bright and curious boy and asked to tutor him.

The priest and the little boy would sit in the quiet churchyard and listen to birds singing. They walked around touching the trees or smelling the flowers. Father Palluy told Louis their names and

Louis never forgot them. Sometimes Father Palluy read aloud to Louis. At home, Louis repeated the stories to the family.

NAPOLEON BONAPARTE

NAPOLEON WAS A FRENCH MILITARY LEADER WHO CONQUERED MUCH OF EUROPE AND BECAME THE EMPEROR OF FRANCE. IN 1814 NAPOLEON'S FORCES WERE DEFEATED BY THE BRITISH AND THEIR ALLIES, AND THE EMPEROR WAS SENT INTO EXILE.

AT ONE POINT DURING THE WAR AGAINST THE FRENCH, RUSSIAN SOLDIERS PASSED THROUGH COUPVRAY. THEY BANGED ON THE BRAILLES' DOOR AND DEMANDED TO SLEEP IN THEIR BEDS AND EAT THEIR FOOD. LOUIS, WHO WAS SIX, MUST HAVE BEEN BEWILDERED AND SCARED BY THESE ROUGH MEN WHO SPOKE A FOREIGN LANGUAGE.

When Louis was seven, Father Palluy convinced the teacher at the village school to let Louis attend classes.

Every day a boy who lived nearby went to the Braille house to walk Louis to school. Louis quickly earned high marks. He spent two years

at the school. He had a wonderful memory and remembered everything that the teacher taught out loud or read to the class. However, it was frustrating when the other students took out their books to read or write.

So Father Palluy went to the Brailles with an
idea. He and Louis's teacher thought that Louis
should attend a special school in Paris. It was
called the Royal Institute for Blind Youth. In all of
France, it was the only school for blind children.

It had been the first of its kind in the world. Louis would have to live in Paris. It would be hard to be separated from their son, but the Brailles wanted the best for Louis. So they agreed that he should go.

Father Palluy climbed up the hill to see the lord of the manor of Coupvray. He was the richest, most powerful person in the village. The

lord wrote a letter to the school in Paris. He asked the director to accept Louis and give him a scholarship. That meant that Louis could go there for free.

The Brailles waited for an answer. At last a letter came. The answer was yes!

VALENTIN HAÜY

ONE SEPTEMBER IN 1771 A YOUNG MAN SAW SOMETHING TERRIBLE THAT WOULD CHANGE HIS LIFE FOREVER. NINE BLIND MEN DRESSED IN RED GOWNS, DUNCE CAPS, AND FAKE GLASSES WERE PLAYING SCRATCHY MUSICAL INSTRUMENTS AT A FAIR IN PARIS UNDER THE "DIRECTION" OF A BLIND CONDUCTOR. THE ROWDY CROWD POKED FUN AT THEM. BUT NOT VALENTIN HAÜY. HE WAS HORRIFIED. "I WILL MAKE THE BLIND READ," HE SAID.

IN 1784 HAÜY STARTED THE ROYAL INSTITUTE FOR BLIND YOUTH, WHERE LOUIS WENT TO SCHOOL AND BECAME A TEACHER. AT THE TIME IT WAS THE ONLY SCHOOL FOR BLIND CHILDREN IN THE COUNTRY.

Chapter 3
A Wider World

On a chilly February morning, ten-year-old Louis said good-bye to his brother and sisters. He hugged his mother, and got onto the stagecoach for Paris with his father. He was leaving his tiny village to go to the capital of France, where more than five hundred thousand people lived.

Four and a half hours later, they arrived. Louis could not see the crowded, noisy streets or the blind beggars on almost every corner. Many of them were children, their hands reaching out for coins. But it must have saddened his father as he held Louis's hand and hurried him along.

To Simon-René's surprise, the Institute was a shabby, run-down building. It was more than two hundred years old. It had once served as a prison. Most of the students were blind like Louis, but there were a few sighted boys living at the school. They took classes in exchange for helping out the blind children.

In a cold, clammy room they met Dr. Sébastien Guillié, the director. He shook Louis's hand, and told him that he would be one of the youngest of the sixty boys in the school. (There were thirty girls as well.) All too soon, it was time for Louis and his father to say good-bye.

A sighted boy took Louis by the hand and led him up a steep flight of stairs to the boys' dormitory. The boy showed him to a bed with a straw mattress and a chest for his clothes.

He gave him a school uniform and a badge. It had the number *70* on it. The boy told Louis to wear the badge at all times.

How strange his new home must have felt that first night. To be so alone and not even be able to see where he was. Louis could hear boys around him talking and laughing. One of them came over and said hello. His name was Gabriel Gauthier. He was just a year older than Louis. They would become friends for life.

Louis didn't know what to expect when he woke up. He quickly found out from Gabriel that if you were late for breakfast, you got into trouble. Dr. Guillié was a stern man who didn't hesitate to punish students harshly. Sometimes he put a misbehaving student in a room alone with only bread and water if he didn't do what he was told!

Louis was homesick for his family and the countryside. He missed the smell of fresh air in the fields and the feel of the warm sun on his face. Here he had to stay inside to study and work. The rooms were damp and cold. Many of the boys had bad coughs.

But Louis was the kind of boy who made the best of any situation. He didn't mind working hard. The other students enjoyed his teasing, easygoing manner. In Coupvray, there were no blind boys to play with. Louis used to sit by himself and listen to the other boys running

around, pushing and shouting. Here he quickly
made lots of friends.

Every morning the boys went to classrooms to start their fifteen-hour day. They studied grammar, arithmetic, history, Greek, Latin, Spanish, algebra, and geography. Learning meant relying on their memories. Louis soon became one of the best students in his class.

Louis had looked forward to using the library. How disappointing to find only fourteen books for the blind there!

These books—with embossed, or raised, letters—used a system invented by Valentin Haüy, the founder of the school. Reading them was slow going.

HOW HAÜY BEGAN EMBOSSING

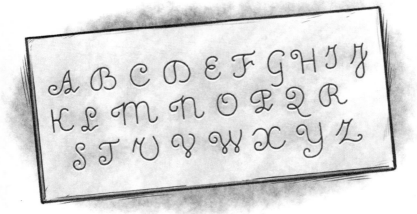

A BLIND BEGGAR, SEVENTEEN-YEAR-OLD FRANÇOIS LE SUEUR BECAME A STUDENT OF VALENTIN HAÜY'S. ONE DAY FRANÇOIS FELT A RAISED LETTER "O" ON THE BACK OF A PRINTED FUNERAL CARD. THAT GAVE VALENTIN THE IDEA OF PRINTING THE ALPHABET WITH EMBOSSED, OR RAISED, LETTERS. BOOKS FOR THE BLIND WERE PUBLISHED. EMBOSSING BECAME THE OFFICIAL FRENCH SYSTEM FOR READING AND WRITING FOR THE BLIND UNTIL 1854.

Afternoons were spent learning a trade. Not
only would the boys leave the school with useful
skills, but their work helped to earn money for the
school. They made many things—woven mats,

fabric for their school uniforms, slippers, baskets,
and fishing nets among them. Again Louis
excelled. By the time he was fourteen, he was
running the slipper workshop.

Although Dr. Guillié was strict and hard to please, he had one love that he shared with his students: music. He was proud of the school orchestra and spent money freely on instruments for the school music program. He even gave the school three pianos for the students' use.

It was Dr. Guillié who discovered Louis's natural talent for music. He could play different instruments by ear. This meant that Louis only had to hear a piece to be able to play it. He played not only the cello but also the piano and later the organ.

Louis joined the school orchestra and the chorus. He played and sang as much as he could. Music would be a part of Louis's life for as long as he lived.

Chapter 4
A Change for the Better

During Louis's second year, a new director took Dr. Guillié's place. Dr. Alexandre Pignier was shocked by what he saw at the Institute. He set about making it a healthier, happier place for the students.

DR. ALEXANDRE PIGNIER

Two doctors examined the children. They were pale and underfed. By now Louis had the same hacking cough as many of the other boys. Some of the children showed signs of tuberculosis, a disease that attacks the lungs.

TUBERCULOSIS

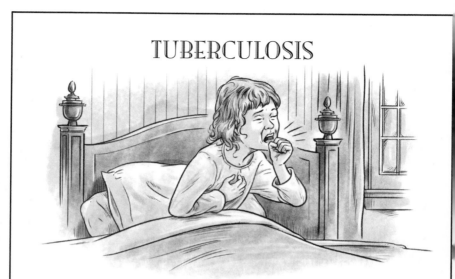

TUBERCULOSIS, OR TB, IS A DISEASE CAUSED BY BACTERIA THAT USUALLY ATTACKS THE LUNGS. TUBERCULOSIS CAN ATTACK OTHER PARTS OF THE BODY AS WELL. IT IS SPREAD THROUGH THE AIR FROM ONE PERSON TO ANOTHER THROUGH COUGHING, SNEEZING, SPEAKING, OR SINGING.

IN LOUIS'S DAY, THERE WAS NO CURE FOR TUBERCULOSIS. MANY BOYS AT THE INSTITUTE SUFFERED FROM TB'S CHRONIC COUGHS. IT WAS EASY TO PASS ON AN AIRBORNE DISEASE WITH SO MANY BOYS LIVING AND SLEEPING IN CROWDED DORMITORIES.

TUBERCULOSIS CAN BE CURED WITH ANTIBIOTICS NOWADAYS, WHICH WERE NOT AVAILABLE IN LOUIS BRAILLE'S TIME.

From the start, Dr. Pignier begged the French government to move the school to a new building. It would take twenty-three years for this to happen.

Dr. Pignier quickly won over the students. He sent them on walks outside the school every Thursday. Fresh air was what they needed. A group of boys held on to a long rope with a sighted boy as the leader. They walked through the Paris streets, taking in all the new sounds and smells on their way to the Garden of Plants.

Louis must have thought of his days with Father Palluy as he smelled the flowers. The boys got to know the gardens well. As soon as they were

through the open iron gates, the boys dropped the
rope and chased after one another, falling to the
grass in mock fights, just like sighted boys.

One summer day Dr. Pignier called the boys together. He had found out that Valentin Haüy was living in Paris in an apartment not far from the school. Haüy had spent years traveling through Europe, encouraging and helping other countries to plan schools for the blind. The frail seventy-six-year-old teacher was almost blind himself now.

Haüy had tried to visit the Institute when Dr. Guillié was the director. But Dr. Guillié had turned him away. Now the school would plan a celebration in honor of Haüy. It took place in August 1821. The students clapped and cheered as Haüy walked into the dining room. He talked with the boys late into the afternoon.

After dinner the orchestra played and a chorus of students sang a song composed by some of Haüy's students thirty-three years earlier. Boys read from the embossed books that Haüy had given to the school when it began.

At the end of the program, Dr. Pignier thanked him for all he had done for the blind, especially the children. Haüy's voice shook as he spoke in a whisper. "My dear children, it is God who has done everything."

Chapter 5
Night Writing

One day Dr. Pignier told the boys about an interesting visitor who had come to the Institute.

Captain Charles Barbier had been an officer in the French army. He had invented a system of reading and writing for soldiers to use in the dark on the battlefields. He called it "night writing." He thought it might work for the blind. He wanted to try it out on the boys at the school.

Dr. Pignier asked the students if they would be willing to test out his system. Now twelve, Louis was probably the first to raise his hand. Perhaps night writing would prove a better way to read than embossed books.

Dr. Pignier explained that this reading system used raised dots and dashes. He passed out a sheet

CAPTAIN CHARLES BARBIER

to each boy and told them to feel the dots.

But how did he make those raised dots? Louis wanted to know.

Captain Barbier came to the Institute to explain. He told them that the raised dots were punched into heavy paper with a pointed tool called a stylus. To read the message, the reader moved his fingers over the pattern of dots.

Then came the harder part. Barbier explained that he had come up with a system of thirty-six basic sounds used in the French language. He arranged the sounds in a square he called a grid, with six rows across and six columns up and down. Each sound could be represented in a twelve-dot cell in two columns.

Louis realized that these simple patterns of dots were much easier to feel than the large curved letters in the library's embossed books. He was eager to learn this reading code.

The boys left the meeting excited about night writing. They needed to memorize the thirty-six sounds in the rows and columns. But the boys weren't worried. They were used to learning through remembering. If they could memorize the grid, they would be able to take notes in their classes and send messages to each other.

Barbier's night writing was definitely a big improvement over embossed letters. Still, it had its

limits. There was no punctuation, no spelling, and
no numbers. Students could write to each other
if they knew the thirty-six sounds. However, they
could not write to sighted people who used the
regular alphabet for reading and writing. Once
blind students left school, night writing would be
of little use in the outside world.

As Louis spent more time using the code with
the other students, he found other things that

didn't work. Maybe he and Barbier could work together to fix night writing. Louis did meet with Barbier. However, the fifty-four-year-old military officer didn't want advice from a twelve-year-old boy.

READING AND WRITING IN THE DARK

CHARLES BARBIER, A RETIRED ARTILLERY OFFICER, HAD SERVED IN THE FRENCH ARMY. HE KNEW THE DANGER OF SOLDIERS BEING SHOT IN THE DARK WHILE READING AN ORDER BY LAMPLIGHT. HIS INTEREST IN LANGUAGE AND HIS WAR EXPERIENCES GAVE HIM THE IDEA FOR A SECRET CODE THAT COULD BE READ IN THE DARK. ARMY ORDERS WERE MOSTLY VERY SHORT, OFTEN A SINGLE WORD SUCH AS "ADVANCE" OR "RETREAT."

BARBIER CREATED A SYSTEM OF RAISED DOTS AND DASHES BASED ON SOUNDS. HE CALLED IT "NIGHT WRITING." SOLDIERS WHO RECEIVED ORDERS IN NIGHT WRITING COULD TOUCH THE MESSAGE AND KNOW WHAT IT MEANT. THEY DIDN'T NEED ANY LIGHT TO READ IT.

WHEN THE ARMY WASN'T INTERESTED, BARBIER THOUGHT IT MIGHT PROVE USEFUL FOR THE BLIND. LATER HE CHANGED THE NAME OF HIS SYSTEM TO SONOGRAPHY. HOWEVER, IT NEVER GAINED WIDE ACCEPTANCE.

Louis wasn't going to give up. When he went home for summer vacation, he was determined that, on his own, he would find an easier way to read and write with dots.

Chapter 6
The Breakthrough

Back home in Coupvray that summer, Louis helped on the farm just as he always had. But whenever there was a break, he worked with his dots. He'd pull out his stylus and a slate with a heavy piece of paper over it. His mother and father would watch as he punched dots into the paper. Then he took the paper and moved his fingers over the raised dots, reading aloud a simple sentence.

Louis explained that the dots represented sounds that could form words. Those words, in turn, could form sentences. He was reading with his fingers. But this system of using sounds was hard to learn, and it couldn't do as much as he wanted.

Later someone wrote that "the good country people [of Coupvray] would smile, perhaps with bemusement, when they saw him pecking at the paper." Monique and Simon-René, however, took Louis's work very seriously. They saw how determined their son was.

By the time summer was over and Louis returned to school, he still hadn't had a breakthrough. But he did not give up. He took his slate and stylus wherever he went, even to bed, so that he could work while the other boys were asleep.

One thing Louis and his friends agreed on: Using twelve-dot cells was too hard. They had to use several fingers to feel the dots. It was

confusing. There was no way to tell where one
sentence ended and another one began.

Louis kept talking over his ideas with his
friends. It took three years before he had a
"eureka" moment. He was fifteen. He thought
that he should try using cells with only six dots.
Then only one finger would be needed to read
the dots. And instead of cells for sounds, his
cells would stand for the letters of the alphabet.

Louis set about creating the alphabet in dots.
It was amazingly simple. Each letter had its own
arrangement of dots in a six-space cell—a cell

made of two columns of three spaces.

The first ten letters, A through J, each had a pattern of dots on rows one and two. There were no dots on row three.

The second ten letters, K through T, each had the same pattern of dots as the first ten letters on rows one and two with an extra dot on row three. When the reader felt the dot on row three, he

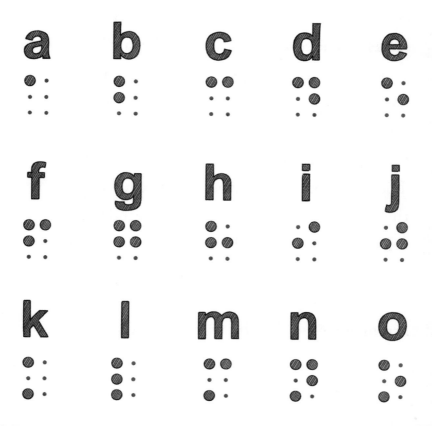

knew he was reading letters K through T.

The remaining letters of the alphabet, U through Z, used the same patterns on rows one and two, but with two dots on row three.

Here was an alphabet that was simple to read and worked for different languages, not just French. A person could write in German, English, Italian, and many more!

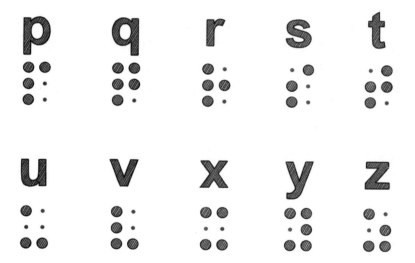

WHERE IS THE W?

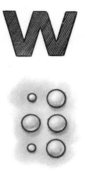

WHEN LOUIS CREATED THE ALPHABET IN HIS RAISED-DOT CODE, HE DIDN'T INCLUDE A *W*. HE MAY NOT HAVE EVEN KNOWN IT EXISTED. IN FRENCH, A *W* WAS ONLY USED FOR FOREIGN CITIES OR A FOREIGN NAME SUCH AS *WASHINGTON* OR *WILLIAM*. LOUIS ADDED THE *W* LATER WHEN AN ENGLISH FRIEND SUGGESTED IT.

Louis was excited. He had found a way for the blind to read and write with ease. He went to Dr. Pignier with his stylus, slate, and paper. He asked him to take out a book and read a part out loud. As Dr. Pignier read, Louis pushed his dots into the paper from right to left. At one point Louis asked Dr. Pignier to read faster. When Dr. Pignier reached the end of a paragraph, he stopped. Right away Louis turned over his paper and moved his finger over the raised dots from left to right. He read back every word that Dr. Pignier had spoken. Dr. Pignier was amazed and proud.

Louis's new method was used in classes. Now it was much easier for students to take notes. No longer did they have to rely on memory to learn their lessons. They could keep a diary and write notes to each other. A sighted person wouldn't have to read books aloud to them. And in the future, it would be possible for any book, no matter how long, to be translated into raised dots.

Louis discovered he could make sixty-three patterns with a six-dot cell. So he didn't stop after creating an alphabet. He made dot patterns for capital letters, numbers, punctuation, and contractions.

Louis designed writing tools similar to the ones Barbier had used. He put a piece of heavy paper onto a slate. Over it he placed a grille with small openings that matched the three lines in his six-dot system. The raised dots were punched into the paper with a blunt stylus. The grille allowed him to place the dots in even lines in exactly the right place.

Later Louis would add math and music symbols to his code. His friend Gabriel must have been especially pleased about the music symbols. Gabriel composed his own music. No longer would he have to keep his original music in his head. Now he could write it down. Others who were blind could play it.

Louis had devoted years to searching for his code. Even so he hadn't neglected his studies. Between the ages of eleven and sixteen, he won prizes in history, geography, grammar, geometry, and algebra. Five of them were first prizes. He was a talented musician, also winning prizes for cello and piano.

Once a visitor at an awards ceremony saw a pile of books on a shelf behind Louis's bench. He was amazed to find out that all the books were prizes Louis had won over the years. He remarked that they "formed a pyramid" much higher than the top of Louis's head when he sat in front of it.

Chapter 7
From Student to Teacher

In 1828 Louis graduated from the Institute. He had lived at the school since he was ten. Dr. Pignier asked him to stay on as a student teacher. Louis's best friend, Gabriel, and another friend and former student, Hippolyte Coltat, had already been student teachers for a year.

Louis must have been thrilled with Dr. Pignier's offer. Now, as a young man of nineteen, he could stay on at the place that had become his home, teaching other blind boys. He remained at the Institute for most of the rest of his life.

For the first time, Louis had his own room. He missed all the noise and fun in the dormitory. But he must have looked forward to having his own private place where he could mull over ideas.

He began thinking about writing down how his raised-dot system worked.

Louis received a small salary. He began saving as much money as he could. With it, he bought a piano for his room.

A FAVORITE PASTIME

LOUIS HAD A REMARKABLE TALENT FOR THE ORGAN. HIS FRIEND HIPPOLYTE CALLED HIS PLAYING "PRECISE, BRILLIANT, AND CASUAL."

LOUIS WAS INVITED TO PLAY THE ORGAN AT A NEARBY CHURCH. HE RECEIVED A SMALL SALARY JUST LIKE THE OTHER BOYS WHO FOUND WORK IN CHURCHES AROUND PARIS.

WHEN GERMAN COMPOSER, PIANIST, AND ORGANIST FELIX MENDELSSOHN HEARD LOUIS PLAY, HE HAD HIGH PRAISE FOR THE TALENTED YOUNG MAN.

Louis became a much-loved teacher among
both the sighted and the blind boys in his classes.
He was generous and kind. If a boy needed
anything, he went to Louis. Even if a boy needed
money, Louis was always ready to give him a loan.

Louis started out teaching geography and

grammar. He taught both blind and sighted
boys. They all looked forward to Louis's classes.
He made the subjects come alive. He could
be lighthearted and fun, but he made sure the
students paid attention. They knew better than to
act up, and most of them didn't want to.

Hippolyte later wrote that Louis's students made "a continuous effort to please their teacher, whom they loved as a respected superior and a wise and enlightened friend overflowing with good advice."

Within five years, Louis, Gabriel, and Hippolyte were promoted. The young men each proudly wore the uniform of a full teacher, complete with gold palm leaves pinned to their lapels.

Louis taught many subjects—geography, history, grammar and spelling, arithmetic, and algebra. Now only blind

boys were in his classes.

In the evenings, he worked on a written explanation of his raised-dot reading system. It was called *Method of Writing Words, Music, and Plainsong by Means of Dots for Use by the Blind and Arranged by Them.* It was published by the Institute in 1829. Louis was quick to credit Captain Barbier as the inventor of the raised-dot code. In his opening pages, Louis wrote: "If we have shown the advantages of our system over that of the inventor, we should say in his honor that it is his system that first gave us the idea of our own."

Dr. Pignier encouraged teachers and students to use Louis's code in classes. It was so successful that Dr. Pignier asked the French government to make it the official method for teaching the blind to read and write.

The answer was no.

The government didn't forbid its use, but

insisted on keeping the old embossed system in place. Louis was sure nobody had even looked at his system. He wrote his own letter to the government, but no one answered it.

In 1834 Paris was hosting a big fair. It was called the Paris Exposition of Industry. Dr. Pignier asked Louis to demonstrate his code there. Visitors from all over the world were coming to see the exhibits and new inventions. Especially popular was the latest steam engine. Many French government officials would be attending. Maybe someone would see Louis using his code and become interested.

Louis sat at a table and when people stopped by, he offered to write down anything they dictated to him. They watched him punch dots into paper as they spoke. What could he be doing? To their surprise, he read back whatever they had said, word for word, by feeling the raised dots.

King Louis-Phillipe of France came by. He, too, asked to see what Louis was doing. He watched and listened patiently, but Louis never heard from the king. Or anyone else.

Chapter 8
A Struggle

When Louis was only twenty-two he received very sad news from his brother. Their father was dangerously ill.

His brother also wrote to Dr. Pignier asking him to look out for Louis. Louis's father and Dr. Pignier had always gotten on well, and his brother knew that Dr. Pignier was already like a second father to Louis.

Louis's father died on May 31, 1831.

That same year, Louis's own health took a turn for the worse. He didn't know what was making him ill. But he probably had the beginning of tuberculosis. Like so many of his students, Louis had suffered from a hacking cough for years. At times he was pale and breathless from climbing

all the winding, worm-eaten stairs at the
Institute.

Louis's health always improved when he
returned to Coupvray. Dr. Pignier encouraged
him to visit often. During one visit he sent Dr.
Pignier a letter about his vacation. "I did manage
to tune a few pianos and if I had been more

enterprising I would have had a lucrative vacation, but I preferred the pleasures of the countryside . . ."

The summers at home always lifted Louis's spirits. He went to the village to see old friends. He walked up the gentle hills as much as he could, enjoying the sun and having time to himself to think.

How wonderful it would be if he could write home from Paris and if his family could write him back. But how could the blind and the sighted write back and forth to each other?

To send a letter, a blind person like Louis had to dictate it to a scribe—someone who would

write down the message. Sometimes this worked fine. Too often a scribe had terrible spelling and poor handwriting, making the letter difficult to read. And when a letter arrived from home, it had to be read aloud to Louis. How much better if the blind could read their letters themselves.

It was no surprise that in 1839 Louis hit upon an idea. He would use raised dots to form the shapes of the letters of the alphabet. The words could be read by the fingers of the blind and by the eyes of the sighted. Louis decided on ten dots instead of six. This was to have room for the letters with tops and bottoms—like an *h* or a *y*.

Once again he used a paper resting on a board covered with a grille of small openings. The letters were pressed into the paper through the openings with a blunt stylus. The letters were made backward so that they could be read on the other side of the paper.

Louis called this way of writing "decapoint,"

or ten-dot writing.

The system worked well, but it took a long time to write a letter by hand. Louis started working with Pierre Foucault, a former student who was also blind. The idea was to build a machine that could do the writing. Pierre was a talented musician and good at mechanical things. He and Louis were a fine pair.

By 1842 they had made the first writing machine for the blind. It was called a raphigraphe. Now the blind could write much faster, and it was easy to use. Although Foucault designed the machine itself, he gave credit to Louis for the idea:

PIERRE FOUCAULT

"My new machine is nothing but the continuation of his discovery."

Louis and Pierre were ahead of their time. It wasn't until 1867 that the first workable typewriter was produced.

Chapter 9
A Dark Cloud

Dr. Pignier was very worried about Louis's health. He was coughing up blood. A doctor was called in. He said that, yes, Louis was suffering from tuberculosis. There was no cure. But a lot of rest could help patients with tuberculosis.

Dr. Pignier urged Louis to cut back on his teaching. He went as far as insisting that Louis return to Coupvray to regain his strength. Louis went reluctantly, but kept in touch with Dr. Pignier by letter.

Sadly, in 1840, during one of Louis's long visits home, Dr. Pignier was forced to retire. His deputy director, Pierre-Armand Dufau, had persuaded the government to get rid of Dr. Pignier and let him take over the Institute.

PIERRE-ARMAND
DUFAU

Louis must have been devastated over the news of Dr. Pignier's departure. Dufau was not well-liked. He was cold and disagreeable. His ideas of how and what should be taught were different from Dr. Pignier's. This meant changes—big changes.

On his return to Paris, Louis found out that there would be no more classes in Latin, history, or geometry. As a teacher he was horrified. But he dared not argue. Dufau might fire Louis, and he wanted to stay and help his students.

Dufau also disliked the embossed type designed by Haüy fifty-six years earlier. He ordered that all the embossed books in the library be taken out and burned. He would replace them with books using systems similar to ones in Scotland and the United States. In truth, they were a little easier to read than Haüy's, but not that much.

One thing was certain: Dufau had no faith in Louis's code. He scoffed at the idea of columns of dots that looked nothing like the actual letters of the alphabet. It didn't matter to him that Louis's raised dots made it faster and easier to read. Any materials or books in Louis's code were destroyed or locked away.

The new school director also forbade the use of Louis's code in the classroom. But the students had no intention of giving it up. They had used it for so long that there was no going back.

So Dufau took away the students' tools for writing the code. Even that didn't stop them. They found ways to punch paper without a slate. They didn't need a stylus. They used knitting needles and nails from the workshops and forks from the dining room.

The older students made sure that the younger boys learned Louis's code. One boy wrote: "We had to learn the alphabet in secret, and when we were caught using it, we were punished."

Fortunately, Dufau hired an open-minded man to be his assistant. His name was Joseph Guadet. He had not worked with the blind before.

However, it wasn't long before he understood the value of Louis's code. He saw the students' determination to keep using it. Guadet was sure the code would find its way to the outside world as the best system for the blind.

JOSEPH GUADET

Guadet just had to find a way to persuade Dufau to bring back Louis's code.

Dufau was a proud man. He wanted all the credit for any successes at the Institute. Guadet suggested that Louis's raised-dot code would probably become the most used system for the blind. Surely Dufau would not get any credit if he didn't allow it at the school where the inventor of the code still lived and taught.

That was all Dufau had to hear. The ban on the raised-dot code was lifted.

Chapter 10
A New Home

All during the time that Dr. Pignier was at the Institute, he had never given up trying to get the government to agree to a new building for the Institute. In 1838, Alphonse de Lamartine, a writer, poet, and politician, had visited the Institute and was horrified at its decaying condition. "No

ALPHONSE DE LAMARTINE

description could give you a true picture of the building, which is small, dirty and gloomy . . . [or] of those torturous, worm-eaten staircases . . . ,"

he told the government. He begged that funds be given to the Institute. They were approved and building began the following year.

Five years later, Louis was at the opening ceremony with his mother and his brother. How proud they must have been. Sadly, his friend and mentor, Dr. Pignier, did not attend.

Guadet showed the audience just how valuable Louis's code was to the blind.

First he sent a blind girl out of the room. Then he handed a book of poems to someone in the audience. While the person read a poem out loud, another blind student from the school took it down with a stylus.

The first girl was called back in. She took what the other blind student had written in dots. Without hesitation, she read aloud the entire poem.

After that, a teacher transcribed a musical phrase. Another student returned to the room and recited it correctly.

Legend has it that a man in the audience

jumped up and refused to believe this wasn't a trick. So he was asked to read whatever he liked. All the man could find in his pocket was a theater ticket.

Again a girl left the
room and the man read
the writing on his ticket
out loud.

Upon her return, the
girl took the paper of raised dots from the other
blind student. She turned it over and ran her
hand over the dots, reading it quickly and without
mistakes. The audience burst into applause.

Guadet must have been pleased. He had great admiration for Louis. His invention of the raised-dot code had helped his young students so much. In a pamphlet about the code, Guadet wrote, "Braille was modest, too modest. Those around him did not appreciate him. . . . We were perhaps the first to give him his proper place in the eyes of the public . . . in making known the full significance of his invention."

As for Louis, he kept on teaching, but not as many classes. He still needed to spend time away from school to rest.

Then in 1847, he began to feel better. He asked to take on more classes. He continued translating books into his raised-dot code. And he enjoyed musical evenings with his friends.

But slowly his health worsened again. After three years, Louis knew he couldn't keep on teaching. He had been battling tuberculosis for more than twenty years. He told the director that he would have to retire. The director understood, but asked Louis to stay on and live at the Institute. In a letter to his mother, Louis wrote: "If the warm weather comes back, the grapes will improve and I will too."

However, in December 1851, Louis had a fierce attack, coughing up blood. He got through Christmas, then he took a turn for the worse. He began to slip away, and on January 6, 1852, with his family and friends around him, Louis Braille died just two days after his forty-third birthday.

Louis was buried alongside his father Simon-René and one of his sisters in the Coupvray cemetery.

He had left instructions on what to do with everything he owned. A wooden box was found in his room. On it were the words "To be burned without opening." Inside were pieces of paper, IOUs, from those who had borrowed money from him. Always generous, Louis didn't want anyone who owed him money to worry about it. Burning the IOUs was his way of saying, "Just forget about it."

It is hard to believe, but there was no mention of his death in the Paris newspapers. The French government was still clinging to embossed letters as the recognized reading and writing system for the blind. However, in 1854, two years after his death, they finally named Louis's code the official system in France for teaching the blind to read and write.

Some twenty-five years later, Louis's code had become known simply as "braille" and was spreading around the world.

In 1952, on the centennial of Louis's death, he was finally honored by his country. His remains were moved from the cemetery at Coupvray to the Pantheon in Paris. A massive domed building, it is the resting place of French heroes.

As his coffin moved through the streets of the
city, a parade of grateful admirers walked behind,
tapping their white canes.

FOR BRAILLE READERS AROUND THE WORLD

MANY WONDERFUL CHILDREN'S BOOKS ARE AVAILABLE IN BRAILLE EDITIONS FOR READERS OF ALL AGES. HERE ARE SOME FAVORITES.

<u>CHARLOTTE'S WEB</u> BY E. B. WHITE

<u>CHARLIE AND THE CHOCOLATE FACTORY</u> BY ROALD DAHL

<u>THE CRICKET IN TIMES SQUARE</u> BY GEORGE SELDEN

<u>SUPERFUDGE</u> BY JUDY BLUME

<u>FANCY NANCY AND THE BOY FROM PARIS</u> BY JANE O'CONNOR

<u>FOREVER AMBER BROWN</u> BY PAULA DANZIGER

<u>GOODNIGHT MOON</u> BY MARGARET WISE BROWN

<u>RAMONA QUIMBY, AGE 8</u> BY BEVERLY CLEARY

<u>SARAH, PLAIN AND TALL</u> BY PATRICIA MACLACHLAN

<u>WHERE THE SIDEWALK ENDS</u> BY SHEL SILVERSTEIN

<u>THE VERY HUNGRY CATERPILLAR</u> BY ERIC CARLE

<u>WHERE THE WILD THINGS ARE</u> BY MAURICE SENDAK

THE HARRY POTTER BOOKS BY J. K. ROWLING

TIMELINE OF
LOUIS BRAILLE'S LIFE

1809 —— Born in Coupvray, France, on January 4

1812 —— Blinded in one eye in an accident in his father's workshop, causing an infection which spread to the other eye

1816 —— Enters the village school at age seven

1819 —— Sent to the Royal Institute for Blind Youth in Paris on February 15

1821 —— Introduced to night writing, a method using raised dots, giving him an idea for a better system

1824 —— Accomplishes his goal of a raised-dot code, eventually called "braille"

1829 —— Completes a book explaining his code and published by the Institute

1833 —— Promoted to full-fledged teacher at the Institute
Hired to play the organ at Saint-Nicolas-des-Champs

1834 —— Exhibits his raised-dot code at the Paris Exposition of Industry

1835 —— Diagnosed with tuberculosis

1839 —— Designs decapoint, a way for the blind and the sighted to correspond with each other

1841 —— Builds a machine he calls a raphigraphe with Foucault, a blind musician and mechanic, which speeds up decapoint

1844 —— Moves to a new building that replaces the Royal Institute for Blind Youth.
Honored at the opening ceremony on February 22

1852 —— Dies of tuberculosis at age forty-three on January 6

1854 —— Braille is finally designated the official system for the blind in France

TIMELINE OF THE WORLD

Abraham Lincoln and Charles Darwin are born on February 12	1809
Washington, DC, is captured and burned by the British during the War of 1812	1814
Napoleon Bonaparte is defeated by the British at the Battle of Waterloo on June 18	1815
Florence Nightingale is born in Florence, Italy, on May 12	1820
President James Monroe declares the Monroe Doctrine	1823
Beginning of the first passenger-carrying railroad in England	1825
The Slavery Abolition Act is passed in the British Empire	1833
American Revolutionary War hero Gilbert du Motier, Marquis de Lafayette, dies in Paris on May 20	1834
Mexico wins the Battle of the Alamo	1836
Victoria is crowned the queen of England on June 20	1837
British scientist Richard Owen invents the term *dinosaur*	1841
Samuel Morse sends the first "official" long-distance telegram between Washington and Baltimore	1844
Gold is discovered in California and the California gold rush begins	1849
Uncle Tom's Cabin by Harriet Beecher Stowe is published Louis Napoleon proclaims himself Napoleon III	1852

BIBLIOGRAPHY

* Davidson, Margaret. **Louis Braille: The Boy Who Invented Books for the Blind**. New York: Scholastic, 1971.

* Donaldson, Madeline. **Louis Braille**. Minneapolis: Lerner, 2007.

* Freedman, Russell. **Out of Darkness: The Story of Louis Braille**. New York: Clarion Books, 1997.

Mellor, C. Michael. **Louis Braille: A Touch of Genius**. Boston: National Braille Press, 2006.

Weygand, Zina. **The Blind in French Society from the Middle Ages to the Century of Louis Braille**. Stanford, California: Stanford University Press, 2009.

* Books for young readers

THE TIME-TRAVELING ADVENTURES OF THE ROBBINS TWINS

THE TREASURE CHEST

"Kids who have outgrown the
'Magic Treehouse' may enjoy this new series."
—*School Library Journal*

Join Felix and Maisie Robbins on their trips through time as they
meet thrilling historical figures as children in *New York Times*
Best-Selling author Ann Hood's *The Treasure Chest*!

www.treasurechestseries.com